THE GOOD NEWS OF JUSTICE

PEACE·AND·JUSTICE·SERIES 4

THE GOOD NEWS OF JUSTICE

Share the Gospel: Live Justly

HUGO ZORRILLA

HERALD PRESS
Scottdale, Pennsylvania
Kitchener, Ontario

Library of Congress Cataloging-in-Publication Data

Zorrilla C., Hugo.
  The good news of justice : share the gospel : live justly /
Hugo Zorrilla.
      p.   cm. — (Peace and justice series : 4)
  Bibliography : p.
  ISBN 0-8361-3473-7 (pbk.)
  1. Christianity and justice.   2. Evangelistic work.   3. Witness
bearing (Christianity)   4. Mennonites—Doctrines.   I. Title.
II. Series.
BR115.J8Z67 1988
241'.4—dc19   88-6903
                                                                    CIP

THE GOOD NEWS OF JUSTICE
Copyright © 1988 by Herald Press, Scottdale, Pa. 15683
        Published simultaneously in Canada by Herald Press,
        Kitchener, Ont. N2G 4M5. All rights reserved.
Library of Congress Catalog Card Number: 88-6903
International Standard Book Number: 0-8361-3473-7
Printed in the United States of America
Cover photo by D. Michael Hostetler
Design by Gwen Stamm

88 89 90 91 92 93 94 95 96 10 9 8 7 6 5 4 3 2 1

To those brothers and sisters
in affluent and materialistic societies
who are living out the justice of God
in solidarity
with the poor of the earth.

Contents

7

Foreword

If you were asked to describe the good life, what would you say? What kind of living leads to fulfillment and happiness, to living justly with the neighbor?

An ancient Hebrew prophet said, "The Lord has told us what is good. What he requires of us is this: to do what is just, to show constant love, and to live in humble fellowship with our God" (Micah 6:8).

Justice, love, and relationship with God form the foundation for satisfying human relationships. Christians, above all, must be concerned about these qualities of life because they express important parts of Jesus' life and teachings.

In this book, author Hugo Zorrilla sketches out the biblical theme of justice for us. He then shows in some detail how this rounded concept of justice plays a vital role in God's good news and how it is shared.

He writes after long study, reflection, teaching, pastoral work, writing, and living in situations of injustice. This includes various countries of South America, Central America, North America, and Spain.

The Good News of Justice is volume four in the Peace

9

and Justice Series listed near the back of the book. Other titles in the series deal with theological, historical, and practical aspects of peace and justice issues. The author also lists in the back several references for further reading.

—*J. Allen Brubaker, Editor*
Peace and Justice Series

Introduction

"Tell me, if the yeast mixed with flour does not transform the dough, would it by chance be yeast? If a perfume does not permeate those that are near it with sweet odor, would we call it perfume? And do not say it is impossible for you to care for others. If you are Christians, it is impossible for you not to care for them. If you say that the Christian cannot be helpful to others, you insult God and you call him a liar."

> —*John Chrysostom, patriarch of Constantinople in the fourth century*

Jesus, quoting the prophet Isaiah, said, "The Spirit of the Lord is upon me, because he has chosen me to bring good news to the poor. He has sent me to proclaim liberty to the captives and recovery of sight to the blind, to set free the oppressed and announce that the time has come when the Lord will save his people" (Luke 4:18-19).

As the church shares this good news, God will be present and will say to his people, "Here am I" (Isaiah 58:9). God will be in the midst of his people, but not because of their religious acts. These are false and offensive when justice is not practiced toward those who suffer injustice. It is only through justice that salvation is made evident. Justice will go before the people and the glory of God will be the rear guard (Isaiah 58:8).

This study deals with the Christian practice of evangelism and how it faces the crippling injustices in our world. Evangelism patterned after the New Testament molds the disciples of the Lord and helps them to see that evangelistic activity and living justly are not opposites.

In biblical evangelism, the announcement of the good news and the practice of justice are integrated. One is not put before the other, nor is either played down. We will see through this study that the gospel is proclaimed by word, but also by acts of justice. Evangelism is a proclamation in both deed and word.

We will first examine the biblical basis for this integrated evangelism. Then we will look at the close relationship between the message of the Word and the "message" communicated through acts of justice. In chapter four, the justice that emerges from evangelism is analyzed. In the final chapter, five, we will study the evangelism that flows from the practice of justice.

I hope that we Christians will seriously live out our obedience to Jesus within the values and guidelines of the kingdom of God. Ordinary believers, as well as evangelists, missionaries, pastors, and mission leaders need to understand the relationship between the gospel and justice.

Too often Christians live without showing the slightest interest in rooting out the problems that destroy human beings. At the same time, however, they expect to evangelize them. Such action is deeply ingrained in the practice of many churches. Some works of "charity" are found, but these often occur only when confronted by great misery and exploitation. In some cases, this help serves only as a gimmick to increase membership lists.

I offer no simple answers or quick solutions to the problems of injustice. Neither do I pretend to give easy "steps" for what is known as personal evangelism. However, I agree with the biblical message: Commitment to the life and teachings of Jesus can be renewed. Consequently, in the evangelizing task, we can confront the injustice suffered, as well as the injustice practiced.

I want to express appreciation to my wife, Norma Esther, for the depth of her participation in the ministry and for her translation of this material into English. The ministry has been a discipleship for me. Also, I acknowledge with gratitude that many of the ideas expressed here were learned in dialogue with the brothers and sisters of the Mennonite Brethren Church in Madrid, Spain. They have been the leaders in a ministry in which reconciliation is sought in the giving of the gospel by the doing of it.

—*Hugo Zorrilla*
Madrid, Spain

THE GOOD NEWS OF JUSTICE

CHAPTER ONE

Good News from the Scriptures— Evangelism as Proclamation

The proclamation of the good news of Jesus is the moving force in all the activities of the church. Christians are acquainted with all kinds of methods, tactics, materials, and evangelistic procedures. Nevertheless, few know the content of this evangelism. They have not clearly understood the gospel.

Some Christians believe evangelism means saying to a friend or a relative, "Will you come to church with me?" or perhaps, "Are you ready to meet God?"

One time two Christians who were doing evangelism confused a member of my congregation. They abruptly approached him in the street with the question, "Do you know Jesus?"

My friend immediately said, "Oh, yes! Tonight I am going to see him. I will tell him you were looking for him."

Jesus, a common first name in our Spanish cultures, was the name of my friend's neighbor. We smile at this incident because of the shallow manner in which evangelism was being done.

One must clearly understand "the gospel" to know how to lead others to Christ and to discipleship in Christian community. We will examine first how the concept *the gospel* appears in the Bible.

Good News from the Old Testament

The gospel (*euaggelion* in Greek) translates from Old Testament Hebrew the announcement of the happy news of victory. The verb *to evangelize*, as well as its counterpart, the noun *gospel*, is frequently used in the Old Testament. This action of announcing the news conveys the idea of happiness or joy in hearing that victory has been declared. Thus, the phrase "declaring the good news" has a positive and joyous message for those who receive the news of triumph.

In spite of opposition from the many nations that Israel encountered, God gave victory to the faithful ones. Even the women brought the news, or words of God's triumph over Israel's enemies. This became the gospel (Psalm 68:11). Hence, the saving work of God (Yahweh) is the joyful news of liberation. This good news has to be proclaimed. We note that the message is closely related to historical events, such as defeat of the Syrian army (2 Kings 7:9ff.; 1 Chronicles 16:23; Psalm 96:2).

In the book of Isaiah, the evangelical proclamation (in the purest sense of the word) has a more ample, universal, as well as future meaning. For the prophet, the good news points to the future, toward a victorious proclamation by the Messiah. This announcement anticipates the kingdom of God (Yahweh's rule) and brings in a new era of peace and reconciliation. It is directed to those who are not at peace, either with God or with their fellow beings. It is for all who find themselves in inhuman conditions (Isaiah 61:1ff.).

Without a doubt, Isaiah understood his duty to evangelize. The content of his good news is summed up simply in this exclamation: "Behold your God!" (Isaiah 40:9). God himself is the one who sends, and the prophet is his messenger or evangelist. At the invitation of God to evangelize the people, the prophet could not resist; he exclaims: "Here am I! Send me" (Isaiah 6:8). Later, it is God himself who affirms his presence in the midst of the people by saying, "Here am I." He was addressing those of Israel who cast their lot with the needy, with the underdog (Isaiah 58:9).

Good News from the New Testament

In the Roman emperor cult of New Testament times, a herald announced the birth of the emperor, his ascension to the throne, or his victories. For the general public, this was the good news of something that had occurred. In the New Testament church, however, the term *gospel* or *good news* loses its secular meaning. The noun *gospel* and the verb to *evangelize* appear early in the church as technical terms without referring to content. When one heard *the gospel*, the meaning was clear. The good news being announced referred to Jesus Christ.

The New Testament sees the truth about Jesus Christ, not as a past event, but rather as a permanent fact. The time of salvation has come, is present, and will be completed in the future. Thus, the gospel (good news) is the event of Jesus who declares the justice of God to the world.

Only Luke uses the term *gospel* in Acts 15:7 and 20:4. Mark does not use the verb *evangelize* at all. Although the words *gospel* and *evangelize* seldom appear in the biblical writings, this does not mean the concept of proclamation does not exist. For example, John uses *the word* or *the testimony* to express the concept. Though the books written by John are often used in evangelism today, neither the fourth Gospel nor the letters by John use the term *gospel* as a noun or *evangelize* as a verb. The exception is found in Revelation 10:7 and 14:6.

Paul is the man of the gospel. He uses the noun form more frequently in general, as well as in the pastoral epistles.

The Meaning of the Gospel and the Action of Evangelizing

The writers of the Gospels center their message in the life and ministry of Jesus. His life, however, was not an ordinary life or ministry. The Gospels begin and end with the announcement: God became human in Jesus Christ. He lived, died, and rose again to reconcile us, thus fulfilling his promise. That is why the writings that reflect this truth are called *gospels*. They announce the good news that Christ fulfilled God's promises. Drawing from what has been said so far, I will try to answer the following questions:

What is the gospel? What does the good news consist of? Very simply, the gospel is Jesus Christ and all that refers to him; it is the announcement that Jesus is Savior. He is Lord. He is Sovereign. Thus, the gospel not only belongs to God, but it comes from him. God originates it. The gospel of the kingdom of God is the news of God bringing his rule

into people's lives. Through faith and obedience to Jesus,
we live under God's rule or in his kingdom. Also, one can
literally say that the kingdom is proclaimed or preached
(Matthew 3:2; 4:23; 9:35; 24:14; Luke 4:43; 8:1; 16:16).

The evangelist Mark uses these expressions to express
the good news: the gospel of Jesus Christ (Mark 1:1), the
gospel of the kingdom of God (Mark 1:14), the gospel
(Mark 1:15). The answer is clear regarding the content of
the evangelistic proclamation: in Jesus the kingdom of God
"became flesh and dwelt among us." In Jesus, the desired
messianic times have been fulfilled. The end times have
begun. As servants and messengers of the kingdom of God,
we not only say that Jesus is Savior, but also that he is the
Lord.

Who is the evangelist or the proclaimer of this good
news? The Gospels clearly show Jesus as the originator of
the promised kingdom of God (Mark 1:14). He begins his
ministry by formally announcing, under the guidance of
the Holy Spirit, the beginning of Messiah's rule in the ac-
ceptable year of the Lord (Luke 4:18ff.). What he says and
what he does identifies him as the one who was to come,
that is, the Messiah (Matthew 11:5; Luke 7:22).

The assignment of proclaiming the message also
emerges from the Gospels. The disciples and the followers
of Jesus were to proclaim the gospel to all peoples (Mark
13:10), to the whole world (Matthew 24:14; 26:13; 28:19).
Therefore, the ministry of Jesus and of his disciples is defined with the verb *evangelize*. With this, they "preached
the gospel" and "proclaimed the good news" in the towns
and the waysides, in words and in deeds (Luke 10:1ff.;
20:1).

As I mentioned before, the Gospel of John never uses the

word *gospel* nor the verb *evangelize*. John's audience understood the fuller concept that the spoken word involves one's life as a whole. This is expressed with the term *testimony*. The synonym for *testimony* (in Greek *marturia*, i.e., martyr) is "the word of God"—the news of the kingdom of God. This idea was also communicated in John with the concept of everlasting life. A true disciple of Jesus remains in the Word. At the same time, to be a true disciple means remaining or abiding in his love. To do this, one must hate the darkness of the world and keep God's commandments (John 8:31; 10:27; 15:10).

Luke also expresses this idea. He believed the events of Jesus' life are shown in the life of the evangelizer or the witness (Acts 1:8; 4:13; 4:31; 28:31). Jesus' word is gospel because it is the explanation of the love of the Father. Anyone who knows him, believes him. Anyone who believes him has come to him. Anyone who has come to him, has received him. Such a person, therefore, has been converted into a child of God and is one who knows the love of God. God being made human makes possible the true sovereignty of God in the life of each person. This life-changing event becomes the good news which is proclaimed (1 John 1:1ff.).

How is evangelism or the proclaiming of salvation done? We have looked at the gospel as an announcement, a proclamation. It is clear in the life of Jesus that his ministry was identified by the verb *evangelize*. He goes to the villages *evangelizing* or announcing the kingdom of God (Luke 7:22; 8:1; 20:1). The activity of Jesus to evangelize is not separated from the announcement of the kingdom of God. Consequently, it does not rest only in words but also in deeds and signs that show the new era of salvation.

Evangelism is generally seen in the church today as the work of specialists or of "communication technicians" or as the art of persuasion. Although God gives gifts to the church, and one is that of evangelist, this gift does not create a privileged elite. Further, it by no means removes responsibility for evangelism from all believers. And more important, the evangelizing message itself cannot be separated from the whole message of Jesus Christ.

The spoken word is essential in evangelism. This proclamation has as its object the life of Jesus and his marvelous works as Messiah. These are works of peace, justice, and love which restore and regenerate every human being. From the beginning, the church saw in the great commission of Jesus the responsibility to live and to speak the gospel. For the first Christians, it was clear that the proclamation of the gospel of the kingdom manifested two forms of expression: words and deeds, proclamation, and performance.

These words and deeds in transformed lives expose the power of God in the darkness of human injustice (Mark 8:35; Matthew 4:23; 9:35; Luke 9:1-9; 10:9; John 10:25; 11:47; Acts 4:8; 6:8; 8:12-13, 40). It is not just a matter of evangelistic words but also of evangelistic actions. It is not a matter of eloquence of speech, but of authority. Words and works should not be divorced in evangelism (John 14:10-12). Such a separation weakens the full scope of the gospel and makes it more difficult for believers to include a spoken witness in their daily lives.

To whom is the evangelistic task directed? The answer seems obvious: to the unbelieving person. We sometimes may suggest or imply, however, that the gospel is directed to unbelievers only and not to us. Someone may calmly say that the gospel is for the unconverted, the sinners, the pagans. Actually, it is for everyone, including us who believe.

According to the Gospels, those who benefited most from the gospel were the people who looked for the coming of the Messiah. These persons were sinners (Luke 15:1ff.; 18:9-14; Matthew 21:31) and often Gentiles, such as the Roman centurion or the woman of Tyre and Sidon (Matthew 8:10ff.; 15:21-28). God also put special emphasis in getting this good news to the poor (Mark 10:17-23; Matthew 5:3; 11:5; Luke 4:18ff.). It seems somewhat unusual that the gospel should have benefited most persons on the edge of Jewish faith.

On the other hand, the proclamation of the good news fulfills a cleansing, upbuilding function for those who want to follow the Lord. A classic example is Revelation 3:20: "Listen! I stand at the door and knock; if anyone hears my voice and opens the door, I will come into his house and eat with him, and he will eat with me." This verse is usually used to refer to the unbeliever. The original message is lost, because it is quoted out of context. When we examine the context, we quickly see that the message is directed primarily to Christians, and specifically to the church at Laodicea: those who hear Christ's voice, open the door, welcome him in, and enjoy his fellowship, the writer says. This fellowship becomes part of the purifying, edifying function for believers.

The gospel also touches the evangelizer. The gospel does not go in just one direction, going out into the world. It also goes inward, toward the people of God who should live out the teachings of the gospel. That is why one must be humble. We must be as little ones, as children (Luke 9:48; 10:21; Matthew 11:25).

CHAPTER TWO

Good News from a New Life— Evangelism as Lifestyle

Perhaps no one understood better the meaning of the gospel than the apostle Paul. When struck down on the Damascus Road and called to follow Jesus, he truly began a new life. His old life of killing Christians ended and he began to live a life of joy and peace. His letters, and the richness of the tone in them, show his understanding of the gospel. We shall study how the apostle to the Gentiles understood evangelism, both its content and its meaning for daily living.

Good News in the Writings of Paul

What is the content of Pauline evangelism? We saw in Chapter 1 that the gospel is not a new teaching, because the Old Testament also spoke of *gospel*. It had a little different meaning there, though, than in the New Testament.

Here it means a fresh, regenerated being, walking in newness of life (Romans 6:4). The proclamation—or testimony of Paul—is Jesus Christ and his death on the cross (1 Corinthians 2:2). In this sense, Paul's evangelism is not the telling of a story, nor the account of the history of salvation. Rather, his evangelism introduces a person, Jesus Christ. He is the central figure (2 Corinthians 4:5-6). Paul's evangelism therefore focuses on Jesus and demonstrates the new life in Christ Jesus.

For Paul, however, the gospel of Jesus Christ shows an unmistakable connection with the covenant of God in the Old Testament. The fulfillment of the kingdom of God in Jesus Christ does not rupture the promises of God, but, rather, fulfills them. Thus, the content of the gospel becomes the fulfillment of time in Jesus (Galatians 4:4-7) and the fulfillment of Scripture (1 Corinthians 15:3).

The gospel is not a formal declaration of opinion on a complex theological concept. On the contrary, it is the proclamation of an event announced by God and in his name. Since this proclamation centered around the person of Jesus, he becomes the content of the gospel. He fulfilled the promises of God announced by the prophets long ago. This historical Jesus, being the Son of God, died and rose again for our redemption (Romans 1:1ff.; 1 Corinthians 15:1ff.). The new aspect was that Jesus changed sickness into health, enmity into reconciliation, darkness into light, death into life.

How does Paul define the message or proclamation of the good news? To answer this question, we must understand Paul's basic train of thought. The fundamental idea of solidarity or group-oneness is ingrained in Jewish culture, and Paul makes this the central nerve of his teaching.

The actions of one member affect the whole community to which he or she belongs. This is known as corporate or representative solidarity. For example, what one member of the family does, in one way or another affects all the members. If the leader of a nation is insulted, especially by the leader of another country, all the citizens of that nation feel referred to directly and offended.

Today, many of us do not experience broad community relationships. Modern life tends to make us selfish and individualistic. These attitudes and motives drive us to live independently of others and for individual benefits. Although Paul does not lose the perspective of each person, he reminds us that we do not live by ourselves. Each person exists as a member of a society, of a body, of a community. In a more universal sense, Paul reminds us that all are made sinners in the first Adam. The image of God in us has been tarnished or disfigured by sin. The grace of God, however, is evident in this same universal sense. In the second Adam, that is, in Christ, God reconciled us, put life into us, justified us, and has made us a new creation (Romans 5:12ff.; 1 Corinthians 1:30; 15:22; 2 Corinthians 5:14ff.).

It is obvious that Paul defined the gospel in terms of the relationship of God with humanity, and of people among themselves. This relationship underlies the saving character of the message. We can see the richness and variety of the gospel in which Paul boasts by examining his definitions of the gospel. The following phrases are examples of how he defined the gospel (RSV):

1. The gospel of Christ (Romans 15:19; 1 Corinthians 9:12,18; 2 Corinthians 2:12; Philippians 1:27)

2. The gospel of our Lord Jesus Christ (2 Thessalonians 1:8)

3. The gospel of his Son (Romans 1:9)

4. The gospel of God (Romans 1:1; 15:16; 1 Thessalonians 2:2)

5. The gospel of the glory of Christ (2 Corinthians 4:4)

6. The gospel of the unsearchable riches of God (Ephesians 3:8)

7. The glorious gospel of the blessed God (1 Timothy 1:11)

8. The gospel of your salvation (Ephesians 1:13)

9. The gospel of peace (Ephesians 6:15)

10. The gospel which was preached by me (Galatians 1:11)

11. Our gospel (2 Corinthians 4:3; 1 Thessalonians 1:5; 2 Thessalonians 2:14)

12. My gospel (Romans 16:25; 2 Timothy 2:8)

13. The gospel (1 Corinthians 9:14; Ephesians 3:6)

It is worth remembering, on the other hand, the diverse understandings Paul uses to identify the gospel he announces. All of them take their consistency and historic meaning in the person of Jesus Christ. The way of the cross is new life for Paul, but an offense (a scandal) for the unjust. The cross is his power, and he is not ashamed to be its servant. The following phrases serve as synonyms of the evangelistic message (RSV):

1. The word of the cross (1 Corinthians 1:18)

2. The word of faith (Romans 10:8; 2 Timothy 4:6)

3. The word of the Lord (1 Thessalonians 1:8; 2 Thessalonians 3:1)

4. The word of God (1 Thessalonians 2:13; Colossians 1:25; 1 Timothy 4:5)

5. The preaching of Jesus Christ (Romans 16:25)

6. All the counsel of God (Acts 20:27)

7. The mystery of Christ (Ephesians 3:4)

8. The sound words (1 Timothy 6:3; 2 Timothy 1:13)

9. The truth entrusted (2 Timothy 1:14)

I have noted already that biblical evangelism binds together how we live with what we say. Even though this truth is clear in the Gospels, church tradition has often made the gospel in Paul's writings a process of mere words. Could this be the reason some Christians feel comfortable with the translation of 1 Corinthians 9:16 (*euaggelizai*) as *I preach* rather than *I evangelize*? The latter suggests living the good news as well as speaking it. Giving more weight to the preaching of the Word than to the living of it, creates an imbalance in the Christian testimony. It also reduces the importance of the living of the gospel by every believer who gives a Christian testimony even though not a preacher. To the Romans, Paul expresses that he glories in having spoken in "words and deeds" (Romans 15:18).

Is the gospel only words? It is evident that for Paul the Christian testimony as a whole is not just proclamation. Words are supported and reinforced with a life of service, with an evangelistic ministry. It is so much so, that the apostle sees the gospel with other qualifying phrases such as (RSV):

1. The power of God (Romans 1:16)

2. Service of reconciliation (2 Corinthians 5:18)

3. Message of reconciliation (2 Corinthians 5:19)

4. The righteousness of God revealed (Romans 1:17)

5. This gracious work (2 Corinthians 8:6)

6. The signs of a true apostle (2 Corinthians 12:12)

The apostle Paul should be seen as someone who not only preached but who also put his life at the service of others. And he did this for the love of the gospel in Christ.

After he became a Christian, he sought to imitate Christ in all of life. His work as an evangelist was backed up by his Christian walk, and he desired that the believers would live and walk as children of light. They also should present their bodies as instruments of righteousness, of what is right or just (Ephesians 4:1; 5:2, 8; Romans 6:13; 12:1-2; 13:9-10).

How is evangelism carried out, according to Paul? Is it different from what is revealed in the Gospels? Paul ties evangelism so closely to the proclamation that it shows the function of the church's witness. By means of the spoken word and works of justice in the world, evangelism addresses the whole person. Paul centers this evangelism in the crucifixion and resurrection of Christ. He thereby shows that evangelism communicates a message of victory—the certainty of triumph over evil and the creation of a new heaven and a new earth where the justice of God dwells.

For the apostle, as well as for all the New Testament, the gospel is spoken, is proclaimed, is listened to, is shown, is made known, is obeyed, is believed, is confirmed, is lived (1 Thessalonians 2:2; Galatians 1:11; Romans 10:8-17; Philippians 1:7, 16). While the spoken word of the gospel is important for Paul, the presence of the messenger with his life and his deeds is equally important. The walk and the words are so closely united that the people cannot deny what they "hear" and what they "see."

In Paul, we find no easy formulas to win people to the Christian way. We find no prescriptions for using Scripture verses as Band-Aids for people's wounds and hurts. Evangelism in the Pauline writings is a well-rounded idea, and its various parts blend into a unified whole.

In Paul's evangelistic methods, he takes the circumstances and the reality of the people to whom he ministers into account. He therefore defines himself as a servant, yet being free, with the interest of reaching some with the gospel: "Among the weak in faith I become weak like one of them, in order to win them. So I become all things to all men, that I may save some of them" (1 Corinthians 9:22). This method of placing oneself into the circumstances of the people far outweighs a Band-Aid-type strategy. Paul lived the gospel and demonstrated its message for all to see, especially unbelievers.

For Paul, both words and deeds are necessary to make the justice of God believable. This justice is seen in a lifestyle that is true to the gospel, and such a life then becomes a living proclamation of salvation. In other words, the one who proclaims salvation should live as his Savior did. Paul speaks of what Christ has done through him by words and deeds, as mentioned above (Romans 15:18-19). Paul reminds the Thessalonians of the same thing: the gospel came to them not only in word, but in power and in surrender of life (1 Thessalonians 1:5—2:16).

Some people seem to think evangelism is done simply by preaching. While this impression continues even today in some churches, it is a partial reading of Paul's evangelistic teaching and practice. This approach evades the responsibility of demonstrating an "evangelical" style of living. Also, preaching relies more upon the techniques of persuasion than on building a relationship with the people who suffer injustice. At the same time, it permits the one doing the talking to ease his own conscience, and to soften the strong message of the gospel which denounces all injustice as sin.

We should note'here that Paul does call those who suffer persecution for their faith to do so patiently as good soldiers of Jesus Christ (2 Timothy 2: 3-13; 1 Timothy 1:8-12). He spoke out of the context of his own trials and imprisonment for the sake of the gospel. Even servants (slaves) who became Christians were called to be honest and respectful, as befits servants of Christ (Titus 2:9-10). By this good behavior they would communicate the good news to their masters.

Good News in the Other Epistles

The emphasis given above to Paul does not discredit what the other New Testament writers state in regard to the gospel. As a rule, the other letters do not separate the salvation proclaimed from the message lived. It is worth noting that the term *gospel* does not appear in the Epistles as a noun. Only Peter mentions *the gospel of God* (1 Peter 4:17). The verb *evangelize* is used more, as are synonyms such as, testify, preach, keep (Hebrews 2:3-4; 4:2,6; 1 Peter 1:11-12,25; 2:9; 4:6; 1 John 1:3-5; 4:14; 5:2). Again, as in the Pauline letters, we notice that the proclamation of the Word goes hand-in-hand with the living out of that message in daily life. Thus, testifying is done with deeds and actions, and one is exhorted to be a doer of the Word (1 John 3:18; James 1:22).

Although the noun *gospel* is not mentioned in these Epistles, that does not mean they are void of evangelistic content. Rather, these letters show that faith in the life, death, and resurrection of Christ creates new life for all who obey him and his teaching. Therefore, the gospel is defined as the incarnated Word or the Word planted in the believers. The list of Pauline expressions for the gospel given earlier can be compared with the following list from the general Epistles (RSV):

1. The word of God (Hebrews 4:12; 1 Peter 1:23; 1 John 2:14)
2. The word of righteousness (Hebrews 5:13)
3. The word of exhortation (Hebrews 13:22)
4. The goodness of the word of God (Hebrews 6:5)
5. The word of truth (James 1:18)
6. The implanted word (James 1:21)
7. The perfect law (James 1:25)
8. The law of liberty (James 2:12)
9. The prophetic word (2 Peter 1:19)
10. The way of righteousness (2 Peter 2:21)
11. The testimony (1 John 5:9-10)
12. The commandments (1 John 2:3; 5:2)

The total task of evangelism, as we have seen, is an integrated whole. It is the job of every believer. Each must show in his or her transformed person the life of Christ, as well as speak of him. Each Christian thereby shows the work and concern of God, not to gain popularity, nor to earn merits, but because the believer offers everyone the sovereign love of God.

The gospel demands faith of the one who evangelizes and of those who are evangelized. It is faith that brings both to rest confidently on the justice of God. Faith, then, produces obedience. This obedience, required of all believers, elevates the gospel and links the way of new life in the kingdom of God with the power of his Spirit. Since this is true, then, we see that evangelism is much more than crusades, campaigns, and "efforts" to change another's religion. It is the service of suffering (*diakonia*) by the mercies of God.

Finally, to bring together all that I have said to this point, let me emphasize the following:

1. Evangelism is a process. It begins with an encounter with Christ and continues throughout life. It is not an isolated point, but a continuous walk of faith and discipleship. In this pilgrimage of faith, God confirms that he has begun our salvation and he continues perfecting it (1 Corinthians 1:18; 15:2; Philippians 1:3-6; 2:12; Colossians 1:23).

2. In this process of evangelism, the grace of God reaches the believer, and because of this fact, Christ lives in him or her. Thus, the Christian's life becomes light, salt, and a sign of the peace of God and of the justice of his kingdom in the midst of the injustices of the world (Romans 1:2; Colossians 1:9ff.).

3. The word *evangelism* also has a character and a tone of exhortation. That is, evangelism stirs up and moves the believer to action. Because of this, all those who have already tasted of peace in Christ discover a call to evangelize. (1 Corinthians 16:13; 2 Corinthians 9:5-7; Ephesians 6:18). In other words, believers carry an ongoing assignment to evangelize, both self and others. It is not to be "preached" exclusively to the unbelievers, but must continue to be good news to the believer.

CHAPTER THREE

Justice—
The Cornerstone
of the Gospel

One cannot really grasp the biblical message of evangelism without a mature understanding of justice. Perhaps this is why many churches seem not to care about injustice. They fail to realize that justice is the cornerstone of the gospel.

In the richer countries, too many Christians live indifferently, in spite of a world that is torn apart by crises and injustices. For example, 10 percent of the military expenses of the richer countries in 1986 could have ended hunger in the whole world. In the case of military expenses, the persons in the government are backed by the law. But is this just? Is this humane? Should Christians not speak out on this issue?

As a starting point, let me say that the evangelistic proclamation is the expression and the result of the grace of God. This is rooted concretely in his justice. In turn, justice gives meaning and form to other biblical concepts such as grace, holiness, liberation, faithfulness, mercy, promises of God, covenant of God.

In the Scriptures, the idea of justice (*Sedaqah* in Hebrew, *dikaiosunē* in Greek) has many shades of meaning. This makes justice difficult to understand. Nevertheless, and for the effects of this study, I want to separate the justice of God from what is commonly accepted as justice in society. A separation has to be made between justice and human law. In human relations, one thing may be just and fair, while another thing is legal. Too many Christians will defend certain behavior because it is legal even though it may be unjust. An example is that of paying for military expenses (taxes) while millions of the world's people starve to death.

A few years ago, I knew of an American woman, who with her family, was a member of a church in the United States. Her husband was the owner of a beautiful plantation of fruit trees. This farm had permitted them to live a comfortable life, with no financial problems in the family. During the summer, this woman worked as a temporary harvest worker, although she was not in need of this work. She had everything she could have wanted. At the same time, others were out of work and needed a job. Worst of all, after the harvest, she applied for and received her unemployment checks.

She was reminded that her actions lacked Christian compassion, especially since so many people in the area were unemployed. She replied, "It's all legal. I am not doing anything against the law. And besides, I think it's fair because I'm the one who worked in the harvest. I don't see anything unchristian about that."

Yes, actually, everything was within the law, but. . . . Today, I still have the question, "Which is more important: justice according to God, or the law according to human beings?" I believe we fall short of the justice of God when we hold two jobs, abuse social-support systems against the well-being of others who have no work, and by doing so accumulate wealth.

Of course, many Christian men and women have suffered in their own flesh because of their commitment to the gospel as justice. In the U.S., citizens have been judged according to the law and jailed for defending homeless Central American refugees and those whose human rights have been stepped on in the name of the law. Also, it doesn't surprise us anymore to know that missionaries have been tortured and killed for that reason in Latin America and Africa. But let us see what the Bible has to say in regard to this topic.

Justice in the Old Testament

Justice in the Scripture, and principally in the Old Testament, is not an abstract concept to ponder. Justice in Bible times was defined in terms of relationships. To understand it, one first has to refer to a just Person, a just God, who exercises justice. Consequently, every person is just, not because of something within himself, but because of right relationships with God and other persons in the community.

The action of being just has to do with the wholesome relationships one has with others. Basically, and although it seems too simple, the issue can be seen in a negative way. Anything that breaks fair relationships is unjust, for it disturbs fair living among people. On the contrary, living out justice promotes community. Defined in this way, to establish justice is to remove everything that hinders healthy relationships between people. To live out justice has to do with resolving conflict so that a community can experience peace and harmony.

The Scriptures clearly show that justice is closely related to faithfulness. In the history of the covenant of God with Old Testament Israel, justice joins with the merciful grace of God. The biblical authors, especially the prophets and the psalmists, show the practice of justice as a dynamic process of the work of God with his people. In response, God demands that people be just with him and with their fellow beings. In this way, "to work as a just person," and "being just," can be underlined.

One can say that someone is just because of the way he or she lives, and not by what each says or because of the influence or the money each has. For this reason, justice includes: an inner motivation to practice good (Psalm 99:4; Hosea 2:2; Isaiah 33:5), a response by human beings to God's love and mercy (Psalm 40:10f.; 89:15-17), just actions that permit true worship (Psalm 118:19; 24:5; 68:3f.), and God's enabling to reestablish just relationships with others (Psalm 7:7f.; 17:13-15).

Grace and justice came to have similar meanings. They bring out various aspects necessary to understand justice with more depth (see Psalm 36:11; 103:6; 40:10; 70:3; Micah 6:5). Grace and justice include: a communal or collective aspect, a relational aspect, a dynamic or practical aspect, and a liberating or saving aspect.

Justice as the Grace or Compassion of God

God's provision of salvation for all human beings is first described in Genesis. Then the idea developed of the faithfulness of God to his covenant with his people in love. The concept of justice gained force in the liberation from Egypt. In time, the Exodus experience came to define God's justice as shown by God's dealing with the Egyptian oppression of the Hebrews.

The Exodus, as a just response of God to the agonizing cry of his people, became a key theme in the entire Old Testament. It is God acting in a consistent manner. God maintained a fair relationship with a covenant people, as had been done in the past and would be done in the future. As a part of the Exodus experience, God asked that the covenant be kept in the relationships among the people. Thus, justice was given a communal aspect.

God not only appears as just and merciful, but as one who is faithful to divine promises. In the midst of the people's agony, God remembers the covenant with Abraham, Isaac, and Jacob. God became aware of the injustice because of the wailing of the oppressed. God participates with those who suffer from exploitation.

God chose Israel and established a relationship of justice not because Israel was a great people, but because God loved them and kept covenant with them (Exodus 2:23ff.; Deuteronomy 7:6-8). Insignificant as they were of all the peoples of the earth, Yahweh (God) loved them and made them a special treasure.

Long before in the desert, facing Mt. Sinai, Yahweh proposed to establish a covenant of right relationships. At the same time, the people under the leadership of Moses promised to listen to Yahweh and to live the commandments of God (Exodus 19:3-8; 24:3).

For faithfulness to these promises, Yahweh does justice and establishes a new, liberating relationship with those who accept divine guidance in their pilgrimage (Genesis 12:1ff.; 15:13; 17:1ff.). The Bible shows us a rich understanding of justice. First, justice means a healthy relationship with God. Then justice is defined in the treatment of fellow beings, especially the poor, the unprotected, the exploited, the widow, and the orphan.

Justice as Loyalty to God

Justice demonstrates loyalty to God. This truth is clearly seen in the various messages of the prophets during the divided kingdoms of Israel and Judah. The book of Proverbs says, "Do what is right and fair; that pleases the Lord more than bringing him sacrifices" (Proverbs 21:3). The biblical sage does not intend to reject the worship of God. The emphasis rests on the fact that sacrifices are of no value when unjust relationships with one's fellow beings exist. Worship will be more sincere and pure when backed by a just life. Thus, God watches over the good and the evil (Proverbs 15:3).

This same justice which gauges true worship serves to identify the wise and the depth of their loyalty. They are just because they are wise, and wise because they are just, living in service to the needy and the poor (Proverbs 8:15-20; 29:7; 31:9).

The prophet Isaiah sees justice as a gift from God (Isaiah 45:8; 61:11), which is made evident by a just way of life (Isaiah 1:17; 58:2f.). A touching but sad note is presented in the parable of the vineyard in Isaiah 5:1-7. The prophet describes the tenderness with which God treated his people, but the result is the opposite of what was expected. God had hoped for upright living, but crime appears. God had expected justice and, lo, the shout of the oppressed.

God speaks out and condemns such injustice.

Amos makes the absence of justice the center of his prophetic accusation against Israel (Amos 5:7; 6:12). The other prophets joined him to denounce the injustice against fellow beings as a bloody form of unbelief and idolatry. The leaders of the nation promoted and participated in the oppression of the poor of the land. Although they didn't reject and renounce the covenant outright, they were still disloyal to God. They acted like the other nations who followed gods that demanded human victims to satisfy their wrath.

Oppression against the poor is an unmistakable sign of ill will and offense to God. He defines himself as a defender of the poor and is loyal to those in need of fair treatment (Micah 1:8-9). This helps us to understand why God rejected all insincere worship and sacrifice, all hypocritical religion: it does not demonstrate fair dealings with one's fellow beings. The prophets clearly warned that a good relationship with God was impossible when fellow beings are being treated unjustly (Hosea 12:5; 10:4, 11-15; Amos 2:6; 5:11; Isaiah 5:23; Micah 6:5-8).

On the eve of the deportation of the people by the Babylonians, prophets like Jeremiah and Ezekiel saw justice from the perspective of loyalty to God (Jeremiah 3:11; 12:1; 22:3; Ezekiel 16:51). Although the people were taken into captivity, God, who is faithful to his covenant, preserves a remnant of the people who are faithful. The prophetic messages that call the people to return to God and renew their covenant with him show that conversion is necessary. This return to God is intended to establish the justice of God. Conversion, therefore, becomes the way to return to a just relationship with God. Conversion makes justice personal and involves us in the establishment of justice (Jeremiah 4:1; Zephaniah 2:3; Ezekiel 14:14; 18:5-9, 14-17, 20; Habakkuk 2:4).

The concept of justice also includes faithfulness to the statutes of God. In other words, a just person is faithful to God. He is faithful to God in that he lives and practices just and fair relations. Habakkuk (2:4) tells the people, "Those who are evil will not survive, but those who are righteous [just] will live because they are faithful to God."

Justice requires faithfulness to the demands of God. Israel's unfaithfulness, however, led to injustice and the need for a new covenant (Hosea 2:20-25; Isaiah 9:6; 11:4-9; 16:5). But at the same time, through the light of faithful prophets, God continued to call Israel to just and righteous living. It would, of course, be brought into fuller reality in the age of the Messiah (Isaiah 59:14, 16-17; Amos 5:21, 24; Jeremiah 31:31ff.). Because the unjust, oppressive behavior among human beings proved the old covenant didn't work very well, God promised a new covenant. This new covenant, which established the justice of God, was begun with the saving life of Jesus Christ.

Justice in the New Testament

With the coming of Jesus and his ministry, justice takes a great turn. The just person comes to be the one who is faithful to God. But the question arises, what does being faithful to God mean? The answer to this question must build on what God teaches in the Old Testament. This includes the fulfillment of his promises in Christ.

From the Life of Jesus

According to Jesus, the just (or righteous) person

gives concrete form to justice. Such a person embodies justice because he or she is faithful to God. This faithfulness is demonstrated in the way commitment to Christ is lived out. That is to say, this commitment is faithful to the extent that it meets the requirements of the kingdom of God.

In the Gospels, the one who believes in Christ is the just one. This person has had an encounter with Christ—has come to him and received him by faith as Savior and Lord. This believing is not a rare, superficial, private, and mere internal change of belief. Rather, this faith brings with it a change of life and behavior in line with the teachings of Jesus. For Jesus, justice is not a magic formula of written or oral instruction. Christ demands that his teachings be lived out in the believer. The just person, therefore, is the one who practices justice because of the Spirit of Christ living within him or her.

Faith is not merely "an acceptance," as in dealing with a concept or an idea. It is not an option only, nor a requirement, but rather a gift from God. From this gift of faith, new life issues from the life of Jesus. From this new life arises the desire to live justly before God and humankind. This living is rooted in a desire to share the love of God, and not in selfish efforts to promote human welfare.

In the Gospel of Matthew, justice is defined as freedom from sin (Matthew 6:12; 18:23-25; 23:23). Matthew uses this definition to contrast the distorted justice of the Pharisees and the justice of Jesus. The legalisms of the Pharisees are opposed to the true justice of the kingdom of God in Christ (Matthew 5:17-48; 6:1-18; 23:1-36).

The justice of God is intimately tied to faith in Christ, as we have already seen. This faith sets in motion Christ's transforming power: from sin to grace, from injustice to justice. Justice also suggests an element of following, of searching for. Justice becomes a goal that one tries to reach through life in Christ. This introduces an element of hope to accompany the judgment that has begun in Christ.

If this is true—and I believe it is—perhaps it is better understood why Luke puts justice within the field of the fear of God (Acts 8:33; 10:35). For Luke, living justly results from reverence before the just judgment of God.

Another truth underlined in the Gospels is that the just will suffer. They are sent into a hostile world. They go as sheep in the midst of wolves. Because of God's demands for justice, they will suffer and in many cases even lose their lives. Suffering will be inescapable for those who want to live justly. In fact, one difference between the just and the unjust is this: the unjust are not persecuted in the world while the just ones suffer persecution because of their justice (Matthew 5:10). The hope is that the just one will have the reward of God in everlasting life, while the unjust have their reward now, and later, judgment.

The evangelist John does not disregard the justice of God. He emphasizes life, while the other three Gospel writers emphasize the kingdom of God. In the Gospel of John, Jesus appears as a new Moses. John introduces the Word of God as "become flesh," not as the law of the Pharisees. They look for lawbreakers, yet they do not even keep the law of Moses (John 1:14, 17; 7:19). In Jesus, though, justice and mercy from the Father have arrived. Jesus transformed justice into love for others. Such love is a suffering love which is put into practice (John 16:8,10; 1 John 2:29; 3:7, 16-18). To live this kind of love, one must remain in the love of Christ and in his Word.

The true, genuine disciple shows loyalty to Christ and

keeps his commandments. This is possible only through
sacrificial love to God and to others in the kingdom of God.
This Christian love leads to social commitment. The result
is a range of just, people-to-people relationships that show
faithfulness to Jesus. This reality was not foreign to Peter
nor to James (1 Peter 2:24; 4:14-19; James 1:20; 3:18; 5:6).

From the Ministry of Paul

I believe Christians everywhere would agree that all un-
fair, unjust acts offend God and therefore are sin. An unjust
life, in other words, is a life of sin. The guilty, the wicked,
the evildoer, is unjust. Also, anyone who sins misses the
mark and does not reach the goal. Therefore, when justice
is spoken of, grace and the faithfulness of God must be
kept in mind. In examining the New Testament, and more
directly the writings of Paul, the sense of sin dare not be
lost. One who does not have the justice of God has failed,
has erred from the goal. He or she deviates from Christ's
established way of behaving. Consequently, he or she has
sinned.

The idea of justice is found at the heart of Paul's concept
of grace. Seen from this perspective, we can say that justice
is a concept of salvation (Romans 3:21-24). Grace and justice express the same reality of God's action in favor of humanity. The cross of Christ has opened the channel to salvation. Therefore, faith and grace have their parallel in
faith and justice. To reject faith in Christ is to lose the grace
of God. To have faith in Christ and not practice justice is a
contradiction. You cannot have one without the other. One
cannot be saved, nor have peace with God, if one does not
do justice and practice love through the power of the Spirit
(Romans 14:17). For Paul, faith without just deeds is a

contradiction, possible only in the "old man," in the "carnal man," in the "natural man."

Clearly, for Paul, persons in the kingdom of God live transformed lives through the power of Christ. Persons who live the justice of God offend the wise of the world, the powerful, who confide in their own worldly justice. Persons who live in Christ show justice, peace, and joy to the world as the signs of the kingdom of God among us (Romans 14:17; 1 Corinthians 4:20). Without stretching the truth, the Christian gives justice human form (2 Corinthians 5:21).

Christians have been accustomed to reading Paul in an abstract, idealist way. The message of Paul in particular has been wrapped in Greek influence and the Western, or individualistic, style of being and living. This has caused topics like sin, justice, and salvation to lose the social meanings they have in a communal society.

Too many Christians today read Paul as if he were a Greek thinker, unaware of his profound Jewish and Pharisaic heritage. They limit Paul's writings to the interior of the human being. The Christian life becomes for them a religious practice without any relation to fellow beings or to society, and thus, a selfish faith. Why do I say this? Simply because I see many churches continuing to teach a gospel void of the demands of the kingdom. They are saying in reality that human beings need not live as examples of the justice of Christ.

Justice flows from the saving action of God. We are made just by faith in God's work through Christ (Romans 3:21-22). This justice as lived by "the justified by faith" defines one quality of the relationship with God and with other persons. Not acting justly as the "justified" is to break this communion with God and with humankind. Simply stated, this is sin, and, for Paul, sin is everything contrary to justice (Romans 6:12-23; 2 Corinthians 6:14; Ephesians 4:24).

We can say, then, that Paul's concept of justice expressed different meanings. Although Old Testament meanings of justice can be found in Paul's writings, he emphasizes salvation by faith in Christ. God's faithfulness and mercy, for example, have been included in the life and saving work of Jesus. He is declared "the justice of God" manifested in the flesh (1 Corinthians 1:30). One should remember that justice is a gift and a sovereign declaration of God. This is made effective in every person who claims for himself this being made just in Christ.

God causes the person to be just through Christ, his justice. Further, God desires that one lives this justice according to what is established in the new covenant. God declares the sinner just, so that this sinner-made-just will walk in a new life. By living out justice, the believer lives as one justified. God reaffirms the creative will. By pardoning his creatures, God establishes peace with each person so that each will be a sign of the times of salvation. Each justified person, in turn, is converted into a servant of reconciliation.

Paul also shows that the justice of God stands opposed to the justice of the law of the Pharisees. Paul based his argument on the word of the Old Testament prophets. When faced with the justice of God, human beings try to offer their own self-developed ideas of justice—false appearances of justice that lack genuine care for the poor and lowly. Of course, a justice seen like that is not a gift of God, but the result of the selfish effort of human beings (Romans

9:31; 10:3; Philippians 3:9). This hypocritical justice, although wrapped in the coat of religion, does harm to others and seeks to justify itself (Romans 1:7; 3:22-27; 4:11, 13; 9:30). It also is acquired by the works of the law (Romans 4:2; 10:5; Galatians 2:16,21).

Finally, in the Gospels as well as in Paul's writings, the justice of God is given human form in Christ. At the same time, the Lord entrusts to his followers the task of reconciliation and justification. For this reason, justification is a gift and a declaration that is made effective in human behavior. Such justification is pleasing to God and just or fair before others. Justice is demonstrated as love. This love makes faith in Christ human because it is a love that suffers for others. It was practiced by Jesus, lived by his disciples, and understood by the early Christians.

In summary, justice is the work of God. Justice results from faith. Justice is in the death and resurrection of Christ, and it is suffering love lived out by the believer.

CHAPTER FOUR

Justice—
The Good News
of Evangelism

Individual Christians, and specifically the churches as bodies, talk a lot about evangelism. Naturally, evangelism is the reason for the church's being. Some would even say that without the evangelistic task, the church would not exist. The question is not, does the church evangelize or not? The question is, how do we evangelize? What do we understand by evangelism? More to the point, is evangelism an activity totally separated and divorced from justice?

In the history of the church, much writing has been done to find an adequate answer to these questions. The pendulum has gone from one side to the other: from evangelism as mere words and proclamation, to evangelism as simply a presence without words. It has gone from a gospel of propositions and concepts to a gospel of mere social actions. I believe it is not solely one or the other alone, but both, with neither taking first place over the other.

I see the problem similar to the example of water. Water

is composed of two elements: two parts of hydrogen (H_2) and one of oxygen (O). When I drink water, I drink H_2O, which has the physical and chemical characteristics of water. I would not drink more or less than two parts of hydrogen to one part of oxygen. It would not make sense if I asked for water that had other proportions of "H" or "O," since then it would not be potable water. For example, it could be hydrogen peroxide (H_2O_2), a germ-killer.

This is similar to our experience in giving the gospel. We cause an imbalance by insisting on only one part—words or deeds. One without the other is a halfway gospel.

The concept of evangelism is often based on a theology that does not tell us much. Or when it speaks, it gives a short, narrow idea of the Christian life. In the same manner, it seems easy to talk of the God of justice.

Nevertheless, how difficult it is to practice God's kind of justice in our daily lives! Living out justice as a part of evangelism has caused many Christians to be persecuted, exiled, silenced, and assassinated. Perhaps that is why some evangelists present a "watered-down" gospel, one that doesn't commit us to face the cruel, unjust realities of our society.

What does it mean to evangelize today when thousands of innocent beings die at the hands of the unjust? What impact does the gospel have when 40,000 children die daily of hunger in the poorer countries? Also, what kind of gospel will accept as Christians dictators and government leaders who promote war, blockade towns, invade nations, and deprive other cultures? Why are the churches silent to the tortures and crimes that are done "for God and for the country" or "to defend the Christian values of the West"? What causes oppressive governments to endorse or encourage the famous campaigns of mass evangelism?

These questions about injustice remind me of the testifying presence of Christians in countries like China or Russia. Many of the Christians in these countries suffer injustices because of their faith. Authoritarian governments generally fear the presence of Christians, their testimony of the gospel and their charges of oppression.

Nevertheless, the church has expanded and grown stronger through a "nonprofessional" evangelism. In other words, the church has grown because lay members share their faith as the natural result of their membership in the body of Christ or the community of faith.

On the other hand, I remember the evangelistic campaign of a well-known preacher who went to Managua, Nicaragua. The government of the then dictator Somoza permitted him to use the stadium without cost. Many Christians viewed this gesture as a great blessing. The evangelist, however, never mentioned in his nightly sermons the state of war in which the country was living. Nor did he offer a fair solution to so much injustice from the perspective of a life-changing encounter with Christ and his requirements for life in the kingdom. A few years later, this same evangelist arrived in Guatemala during the government of the dictator, General Rios Montt. In spite of the crimes, tortures, disappearances, and the militarization of national territory, nothing was said about this injustice. At the time, 45 percent of the violent deaths in Latin America were of the Guatemalan people. This preacher, to the surprise of some Christian leaders, made no mention of so much cruelty against the Indian peasants.

Someone might object by saying that this would get the church mixed up in politics. The interesting thing is that this evangelist had words of praise for the dictator Rios Montt, whom he considered a "sincere Christian." Is not this a political position? Besides, to be silent about so many barbaric murders is perhaps to be mixed up in politics already. This is not the place to develop the political implications of evangelism. Let me clarify by saying that I am not talking of the politics of a party, but of the good functioning of a society.

In this sense, both the attitudes and the conduct of Christians have political effects. This includes missionaries who present an image of not being political, of being "neutral." In spite of their stated nonpolitical stance, they often demonstrate a political position which hinders the total gospel. Television ministers face the same problem. For example, in early 1987, a well-known United States TV evangelist conducted a campaign in the soccer stadium of San Salvador. During these evangelistic meetings, he praised the military forces of El Salvador. Weeks before that, in Chile, he said that General Pinochet was "a blessing from God for Chile."

These comfortable positions in evangelism not only sell out the gospel to the powerful, but also convert justice into a private, personal, moral matter—abstract and selfish. The practice of justice is thus reduced to a simple morality, which often imposes on others the values and customs of the dominant cultures. Rather than the justice of God, values of Western (European-North American) cultures are presented as Christian values. This has been done with such an impact and "success" that to be Christian means to imitate the way to dress, to eat, or to talk in London, Paris, Madrid, or New York.

It is encouraging, on the other hand, to know of the

work of many missionaries who are laboring in contexts of injustice. They have come to be the voice of those without a voice, and are teaching a holistic understanding of the gospel. Also, the theological evolution of the well-known evangelist Billy Graham is significant. His messages are more holistic today than two decades ago. That is, they address the needs of the total person more so than in the past.

When the strengths of a political system or the virtues of a cultural form are proclaimed, the message is politics, public relations, and propaganda. The gospel of the kingdom of God, however, is committed to unmask the false values in these. The interests of this world, the life of privilege, and the dehumanizing systems cannot be defended with biblical texts.

People become slaves to evil when a society creates artificial needs that cannot be fulfilled. People begin to steal, kill, or cheat to fill the evil desires that have been created. In many cases, people turn to drugs, gambling, or prostitution. This type of behavior creates independence on "crutches" that make people less than God wants them to be (Romans 1:28ff.).

The life of every person freed in Christ takes on unfamiliar and unusual dimensions for the unbeliever. The mystery of God in human flesh cannot be reduced to an explanation, to rational points of faith. Likewise, justice is not determined only by economical structures, nor by the things that are possessed, nor by the social levels of the industrialized societies. For this reason, the gospel of the kingdom speaks a clear word against individuals and societies that promote and defend the accumulation of riches. The gospel reproves those who manipulate society for their own selfish gain. The gospel denounces those who make the business of war a foundation to maintain economic security for themselves while bringing bloody misery to others.

Comfort, leisure, and waste as set forth by a theology of success and prosperity separate people from God. Persons who advocate this kind of living become a stumbling block for their fellow beings. That is to say, we can have no comfortable, just, Christian life while we think only of ourselves or exploit other human beings. The gospel announces freedom from this new form of economic slavery.

The Kingdom and Work for Justice

Where does the evangelistic task begin? Where does it come from? From God? From the churches? From missionary structures? Or from the world? Whatever answers are given, they must come together in God himself. To fully understand our theme, we must look at the kingdom of God, as Jesus demonstrated it.

I begin by underlining a biblical truth that is seldom taught: Neither the believer nor the churches can be independent of the kingdom of God. All Christian teaching, including the doctrine of the church, cannot stand alone, for it is derived from the kingdom. We remember also Jesus began his ministry announcing not the church, but rather the kingdom of God.

The Biblical Notion of the Kingdom. The idea of God's (Yahweh's) rule over Israel developed during the times of the kings. God ruled over the people and over everything created. Thus, in accord with his merciful covenant, the governors and kings in Israel were to be servants of Yahweh. They were to obey God as king by doing justice to every person according to God's covenant (Psalm 72:1ff.).

When God brought judgment upon the people because of their unfaithfulness to the covenant, the prophets assured them of a glorious future with the reigning of God. For the prophets, this reigning meant the presence of God would come near to the people. God would guide them like a shepherd and reunite them from all the earth under his power and dominion (Ezekiel 34:11ff.; Micah 2:13; 4:7). God would come near to save, not only for the people of biblical Israel. This just rule of God would also be universal, with salvation for all who will follow this new leader as Lord. This reality foreseen by the prophets would come with his Anointed One or Messiah. This Anointed One would bring the good news of liberation to the poor (Isaiah 61:1ff.; Luke 4:18f.). Through the Messiah's liberating work, the poor would be converted into "trees of righteousness" (Isaiah 61:3).

In the New Testament, these expectations are fulfilled. Jesus gave human form to them when he began proclaiming the gospel of the kingdom of God. In this, Jesus clearly agreed with the prophetic proclamation of a righteous God who establishes a new order of things. This beginning of God's rule in Jesus shows that Satan's domination has ended. The kingdom of God now conquers the kingdom of the world by the righteous work of Jesus.

The term *basileia* in the New Testament has to do with royalty, dominion, power, or lordship. It was used in Jesus' day to express the presence of God or his sovereignty in everything created. In Jesus is identified the glory of God, his kingdom, and his person. In Jesus, God is available to human beings for freedom from slavery. Through Christ, we are freed from "the kingdom of this world." The New Testament identifies this kingdom as the sin with which

Satan enslaves with deadly, corrupt power. The kingdom of God, on the other hand, is the creator of life. Under God's power, harmony and salvation are now restored to all of creation.

In Jesus, then, the Old Testament concern for justice is joined with that of the New Testament. Jesus becomes the justice of God by making possible this new kingdom of love and salvation. The Gospels, therefore, speak of God in terms of the kingdom of Jesus. He has and promises a kingdom that is of God and of heaven (Mark 13:41; Ephesians 5:5). Kingdom and royalty, dominion and king are closely united in Jesus. What he says and does are interpreted as a fulfillment of the long-awaited Messiah, as the desired messianic kingdom. In this royal kingdom of Christ, God expresses special concern for the poor, the afflicted, the tortured (Psalm 72:12-14; Luke 4:18-19).

The Message of the Kingdom. With all its force, the kingdom penetrates the imperfect world of humankind. Jesus established a new relationship of values in line with the one God originally wanted with human beings in creation.

Such a relationship demands a return to God—a conversion from injustice to justice, from death to life, from darkness to light. God took human form to destroy the powers that dehumanize. For that reason, evangelism in words and deeds will confront situations of injustice. Even more so, the justice present in the life of the kingdom of God becomes the force for evangelistic activity in the churches.

Jesus does not define with theological explanations what he meant by the gospel of the kingdom. He tried to demonstrate its meaning as he "went everywhere doing good." The multitudes sensed what Jesus wanted to say, and they followed him because God was with him. No one had spoken with so much authority nor had subdued the demons with so much power. All that Jesus did and said reveals the love of God. He evangelized with words and deeds. His miracles spoke of the love of the Father and showed his power to save.

The kingdom, as God's rule over all creation, is greater than the church. The latter is made up of those who are called out to live under God's rule, as begun by Jesus. Many times evangelism is done because the church is considered as the content of the gospel. This is why the church does not tire of preaching to itself. This may explain why some Christians give the kingdom of God only a small part in the teaching of the church. Or they may identify the church as equal to the kingdom. But from the biblical point of view, it is the complete opposite. The church is a part of the kingdom of God and should be its sign in the world. While the first Christians considered the church as something important, they recognized that it began with the message of Jesus regarding his kingdom.

The first Christians therefore made the kingdom the center of their evangelism in words and deeds. Although the kingdom of God is not limited to the church, it is expected to proclaim this reign of God begun with Jesus. He demonstrated the kingdom in his preaching and healing ministry (see Matthew 4:23-25 and 13:1-50).

The Presence of the Kingdom in the Practice of Justice

Many scholars have tried to define evangelism and how the church goes about doing it. In the past decade, we have seen an emphasis in Christian practice on obedience to Jesus. I am convinced that this is not a new direction, but an old one. Sometimes it is abandoned because it does not yield easy results. We must, however, emphasize obedience to Jesus because of the sin and injustice in which countless people exist. The life of Jesus and his signs have great force in the unjust context in which the church ministers.

Since obedience to Jesus as King is important, what is the role of the church in the world today? What is seen as the church? We easily observe church organizations, structures, boards, and commissions, but where is the kingdom? In other words, how do we know that the kingdom of God is with the churches? As more injustice and violence occur in society today, the promise of peace, love, and justice seem more unreal and utopian. Let us pray that the practice of justice by the church will point to the presence of the kingdom.

The Already *of the Kingdom and the* Now *of Christians*

With the words and signs of Jesus, the kingdom *already* has begun. The royal and sovereign dominion of God is in the world now. Although there is an element of the future in the kingdom, with Jesus the just rule of God has begun to unfold. Between his ascension and his return, Jesus has left a time in which Christians must be signs of God's kingdom. This, of course, is not something abstract. Rather, the practice of the Christian has to do directly with the just rule of God. We notice in the Gospels that the words and acts of Jesus bring life, liberty, and salvation to people. In a world marked by social injustice, brutality, superstition, and idolatry, the obedient church will be a sign of hope.

The two disciples sent by John the Baptist asked Jesus:

"Tell us . . . are you the one John said was going to come, or should we expect someone else?" (Matthew 11:3). They wanted to find out if Jesus were the Messiah. If he were not, they could conclude that the kingdom had not yet arrived. If he were the Messiah, the kingdom was then with them. Jesus answered immediately. He called attention to the things that the disciples themselves had seen and heard. What are these things? The healing of the sick, the signs of new life, and the proclamation of the good news to the poor. These are the proofs of the *already* of the kingdom.

God has entered into the history of humankind through Jesus. He is the King in this kingdom. Living obediently in God's kingdom causes changes in human relations. These changes influence human behavior more than political ones. The kingdom introduces a new order of values and attitudes that contrast sharply with those of the world.

If the church is a sign and a messenger to the world with a new style of living, then evangelism should begin at church. That is, the church, in an attitude of conversion, should be the first to abandon the privileges of this world. It should give up the vainglory of being in power with persons the people scoff and jeer. Churches in general should forsake all arrogance, false spirituality, and bureaucratic ambitions. A confession of guilt is needed so that the Holy Spirit can move in liberty.

To live their faith in line with the liberating action of Jesus, their churches should side with the needy. They should decide in favor of those whom Jesus loved—the sinners, the poor, and the exploited. With this in mind, the question, "How are the churches signs of the kingdom in a cruel and unjust world today?" is not a useless one. The be-

havior and the message of Christians should bring the
church to develop new services.

The community of the faithful expresses the life of Jesus
in the world today. It knows the fight is not "against
human beings, but against the wicked spiritual forces in
the heavenly world, the rulers, authorities, and cosmic
powers of this dark age" (Ephesians 6:12). It therefore
should evangelize in actions and in proclamation, in works
and words. It should recognize that it is a prophetic instrument in the hands of God. The *now* of the kingdom which
Jesus began is carried out in people who seek justice. The
church is a part of, a sign of the kingdom. While the
church as a structure and as a human organization can
change and will pass on, the kingdom of God is forever.

The Not Yet *as the Hope of the Christians*

I have explained above that Jesus began the kingdom of
God with his works and his words. Both activities define
the gospel of salvation. God has acted in history with a new
covenant of love. Meanwhile, the church waits in Christ for
the final end of time in the presence of God who will finally
establish justice. Thus, each time the community of believers meets and participates in the Lord's Supper it does so
"until he comes" (1 Corinthians 11:26).

The believer is incorporated into the kingdom, not by
self-merit, but as a gift of God. As a new creation, the believer seeks to do the will of God, to live in communion
with God and in peace with fellow human beings. The
Christian has thus already begun to live the promises of a
new order in Christ. The believer's redemption, therefore,
rests in the presence of the Spirit of Christ. His Spirit serves
as the promise that guarantees a glorious future for the

Christian as Paul says, "Christ is in you . . . the hope of glory" (Colossians 1:27).

Paul's affirmation points toward the future reign of the believers with Christ (Colossians 3:4). They have the hope that the glorified Christ will come to perfect that which has not yet been done in the kingdom. This will be "the day of the Lord," when the community presents itself faithful to the gospel as "a glorious church" (Ephesians 5:27).

No doubt, the evangelist John understood the tension of time in the *now* and the *later* in the life of Jesus: "My time has not come" (John 7:6-7). "Jesus knew that the hour had come" (John 13:1). "In that day . . . I will manifest myself to [you]" (John 14:20-21, RSV). Matthew also gives a vision of the presence of God with the believer, both in the midst of the community and to the end of the age (Matthew 1:23; 18:20; 28:20).

The Lord Jesus himself, on the other hand, gives the assurance that he will come to judge the people "in his throne of glory." Those who have done works of love with their fellow beings, who have evangelized their sister and brother, are the just who will inherit the kingdom. The evangelist Matthew, in his picture of the final judgment, shows us what Jesus desires and demands of his followers (Matthew 25:31-46). Here we see not only that Jesus is the Judge, but we also see the results of his judgment—life or death. The attitude taken toward Jesus and the response to his commands for daily living will decide the definite future of the people. When this text is read, readers often miss an important truth: Jesus has identified with the most needy persons, "the little ones." They are the hungry, the thirsty, the naked, the sick, the prisoners, the homeless. The inescapable question in the final judgment will be

"How have we reacted to those in need of justice?"

The hope of the fulfillment of the promises of Christ is a natural ingredient in evangelism. The church does not proclaim salvation to ease the conscience of people. Rather, it matures believers in order that they might continue to be faithful. The hope is, as the apostle to the Gentiles taught, to "keep on working with fear and trembling to complete your salvation" (Philippians 2:12; 3:12ff.).

Building a relationship with the sinner is vital in evangelism. This brings the Christians who follow Jesus to commit themselves to change unjust situations. From this human context, the church arises from among the ruins of the world. By losing its life, the church brings Jesus near to the persons who suffer injustice. Any proclamation of the gospel must include the necessity of self-denial, or a disposition to "take up the cross daily" (see Matthew 16:24-27).

The most common and traditional method to evangelize is with words only. But this does not exhaust the means that the Spirit gives the church. Following the example of Jesus, the churches must back up their proclamation by helping those who suffer from personal and social sin.

CHAPTER FIVE

Evangelism—
The Good News
of Justice

The previous chapters have provided some of the biblical material necessary for dealing with problems in society today. Earlier chapters also examined the basic contents of evangelism from a global perspective. In the preceding chapter, we noted the necessity for true evangelism to be united with a consistent practice of justice. Now, we want to look at the other side of the coin: the practice of justice has to be evangelistic.

The signs of the kingdom also are messages of the same gospel of God. The specific acts of "doing good," according to the first letter from Peter, are evangelistic events within an unjust situation of sin. Jesus comes near in word and deed. He comes near to persons in sinful situations: publicans, Pharisees, drunks, prostitutes, lepers, foreigners, the impure, the sick, the rejected, the Samaritans. His words of hope and love are lived out in historic actions that make the gospel an integrated truth. That is, actions that create life, as the practice of justice in contexts of oppression, become part of the gospel. Such actions are the good news of salvation or of liberation. The Scriptures teach a gospel that integrates and makes life whole. Evangelism, therefore, is not just a matter of talking. Nor is it a matter of works only. It is both.

What does this total evangelism mean? How is evangelism accomplished by justice? It basically implies a conversion to Jesus, "the justice of God," and to a Christian commitment to live as "trees of justice." Such holistic evangelism has five aspects:

1. It sees the effects of exploitation and injustice through the eyes of the poor.
2. It participates in and feels the cruel anxieties of those who suffer, because of personal sin and because of the sins of others.
3. It denounces unjust practices and structures that impoverish, dehumanize, and kill.
4. It identifies the systems and processes that produce death. Such systems show that abundance for some and poverty, torture, and misery for the majority is not a casual thing, but the result of rational thought. Poverty is usually not voluntary, as if it were a virtue, but is often caused and carried out from centers of power.
5. It sees the gospel of the kingdom to the poor in correct perspective. This good news of justice is for all those who not only have nothing, but who have systematically lost everything, even their hope of a better life.

What kind of evangelism would Jesus practice today? Presently, some 50 wars are going on in the world. Twelve percent of the population of the world lives affluently with 50 percent of the riches of the world. Three percent of the population of Central America owns 75 percent of the most productive land. And 13 percent of the population in South Africa are whites who, supported by some churches, exploit the other races through a brutal and inhuman segregation. Millions of persons die of hunger in the world, while in developed countries food is destroyed to maintain food prices.[1]

In Russia, people continue to be persecuted and tortured because of personal convictions. Many persons support, as though blessed of God, the sale of armaments by their governments to the poor countries, even though this business makes them even poorer. Suicides among young people increase in an alarming way. The external debt of the poor countries can never be paid when interest rates for them are so high. What would Jesus call for in such seemingly hopeless situations? What would Jesus have us to do to establish justice between persons and between peoples? One thing is certain: his kingdom values do not change for his followers, even in situations of personal and corporate sin.

The Evangelist's Key to Understanding Justice

The church knows that it has to be believed in the world. With this credibility, a horizon of possibilities is opened to share the love of Christ with those who suffer. Obviously, one cannot speak of Christ nor live his justice if one has not had a transforming encounter with him. After such a complete change of life, one can testify of the power of God. Without much education in theology, but with great wisdom, one can share what the Lord has done in one's life. The man blind from birth who had an encounter with Jesus could testify to the religious leaders in Jerusalem " . . .

one thing I do know: I was blind, and now I see" (John 9:25).

Who is the active participant in evangelism? How is his or her testimony defined in the church in contrast to those who consider themselves professional evangelists? The gift of evangelist bestowed by the Spirit on some believers is worth remembering. This gift is given among many others but in the immediate context of the community of the faithful. As any other gift, it is given to the church for edification and for service to the world. It is not for personal gain, inside or outside the congregation, much less as a big moneymaking profession. In true evangelical practice, the participant in evangelism is an obedient disciple under the direction of a body of believers.

The life of the Christian is a private and also a communal process, where to believe means to carry out the requirements of the kingdom. Thus, the inseparable unity between what is believed and how that belief is lived out is plainly shown. This affirmation is so important that there cannot be evangelistic action without the gospel proclamation showing through in the way one lives the message. The contrary would be to believe the message without being concerned about what is done or how one lives. This type of evangelism—separating practice from faith—Jesus strongly criticized and denounced. An example is his charge against the scribes and Pharisees. He called them hypocrites. They were willing to travel over land and sea to make a single convert, but their actions were unjust and they shut out the kingdom of heaven against men (see Matthew 23:13-28).

How then does one define an evangelist who practices justice? Who is such a person? How does he or she act?

Declared Just in Christ. Through faith in Christ, the believer is declared just or right with God (Romans 1:17). Each believer has sacrificed life and bodily members as instruments of justice (Romans 6:13; 12:10). Each knows that he or she has passed from death to life. Each also knows that the cleansing fount continues to be open in Christ (1 John 1:8ff.). With neither arrogance nor self-sufficiency, each knows, from the message of Jesus, the need to live the gospel. In other words, each should do good even if it means suffering (Romans 8:17; 1 Peter 3:13ff.; 4:12ff.).

The intimate relationship between faith and the practice of that faith is evident in the ministry of Jesus and that of the New Testament church. The preaching of Jesus and his saving signs and actions were not separated. Both truths are inseparable. In other words, one cannot talk of the faith and live in a manner that is different from that faith. This is how we begin "to do the will of God," or similarly, "to do the justice of God"—by facing oneself and facing the persons who need the gospel. This relationship is an intimate one in regard to "the fruit of justice" of James 3:18, and "the much fruit" of John 15:1ff.: Goodness is the fruit produced from the seeds peacemakers plant in peace.

"You will know them by what they do," Matthew states in 7:16a. This clearly underlines for us the relation between the Christian testimony and the authority of a faith which does the will of the Father (Matthew 7:21).

Still fresh in my mind is a certain experience I had in Madrid, Spain. During a meeting with four well-known preachers there, a question arose. They asked me, "What do you Mennonites believe?"

I showed them the importance of the teaching of the Sermon on the Mount (Matthew 5—7). Jesus taught that it was essential to live what we believed so that the people would believe. I reminded them that Jesus told us, "You will know them by their fruits." I had scarcely finished saying this phrase when the four preachers, almost in unison, emphatically told me, "Oh, no, no. It's not like that—that's not for today." And with that, they changed the topic.

Sadly, a few days later, I found out that of the four evangelists, three had serious ethical problems in their lives. They had no moral authority to announce the gospel, since they were not living it.

The evangelical walk is a life, an evangelical style of living. He who evangelizes with words should do so with his life as well. The words that are proclaimed are not so much *spoken*, as *done* (James 1:22). People are tired of so much talking, so much self-sufficiency in what is said without a Christian practice. This is why the truths of the gospel cannot be reduced to a few phrases or verses taken out of their context, often for the purpose of "winning" an argument. This truth is a practice, a walking in the light. It is a practice of the justice of God (1 John 1:6-7; 2:29; 3:7).

A few years ago in a local church in Cali, Colombia, the believers decided to carry out an evangelizing effort in the neighborhood. This activity permitted more people to come to the temple on Sundays. The congregation entered into a phase of consecration, and some people dedicated their lives to the Lord. One of these persons was a young lady who lived near the temple and was the neighbor of one of the members of that church. One Sunday, as part of the program, opportunity was given to the believers to testify of their encounter with Christ. The young lady gave her testimony. The pastor asked her what part of a sermon, or what Bible verse, had motivated her to make a decision for Christ. She responded, "Frankly, what was preached really didn't impress me. Don't misunderstand me. I didn't come because of what I heard, but I came because of what I saw. I want to say that I live next door to one of your members, and the past several years I have seen that this brother lives what he believes and what he says. It's his life that has spoken to me more than his words."

The words of this young lady continue to be true about speaking of the Lord with Christian humility. It is not how much is said, but how just and fair one lives. Or better yet, it is the way Christ shows through in the life of the believer who in obedience lives close to those who suffer and do not know Christ.

Under the Lordship of Christ. The Christian who knows and has experienced the grace of the Lord acknowledges the lordship of Christ. He establishes justice between God and the believer. Apart from this truth, no evangelism exists. The following three subpoints will help clarify what is meant by the lordship of Christ in the life of the Christian:

First, *be a servant of others.* One must be a follower of Jesus without aspiring for power. In Mark 10:35ff., Jesus answers two of his disciples who desired privileges and power in the kingdom. Jesus taught all twelve disciples that if one of them wants to be great, "he must be the servant of the rest; and if one of you wants to be first, he must be the slave of all." He also foretold suffering for his disciples, similar to what he, their Master, would suffer.

In the same way, it stands out that the one who proclaims is not greater, nor even equal, to the one who sends (John 13:13-17). For the apostle Paul, Christ lived in him, and all that he did, he did in the faith of the Son of God

(Galatians 2:20). Thus, he did not live for himself but for the Lord. For him, living for the Lord was measured by how he served as an instrument of reconciliation (2 Corinthians 5:14ff.).

Second, *be part of a suffering discipleship.* On many occasions the gospel proclamation will encounter injustices, which are sin, and denounce them. This leads those who never want to be converted to the Lord to silence the message (John 12:24-26; 15:18f.). Both the Scripture and experience confirm this truth. Discipleship, therefore, offers not only the blessing of salvation; it also makes us participants in a life of voluntary suffering. Only then are the words of Jesus to "take up your cross daily" understood as a basic condition: first, to come to him in an attitude of surrender and, second, to follow even to death if necessary (Luke 9:23; 14:27).

No doubt the first communities of Christians understood clearly these comments of the gospel. The believers did not try to distort the truth or evade any painful end they might experience. Paul felt he suffered for the Colossians and that his sufferings were part of the afflictions of Christ on behalf of his church (Colossians 1:24ff.). It should be clarified that this way of understanding the lordship of Christ is not an attempt to escape nor to invite persecution. It is rather obedience to Christ as "instruments of justice." It is to participate fully and totally in the demands of the gospel with joy (1 Peter 4:12ff.).

Third, *be guided by the power of the Spirit.* A great truth in the life of the disciple of Jesus is the promise of the coming of his Spirit as Guide and Teacher. Jesus himself breathed the Spirit over the disciples and sent them out just as the Father had sent him (John 20:21-22). This Spirit dwelled in the faithful and believing people, making them his body and his temple. He has come for all those who confess that Jesus is Lord. No one can proclaim this truth if he has not been born again and does not live under the fullness of his Spirit (1 Corinthians 12:3).

"To be in Christ" and "to have the Spirit" are the same thing for Paul (Romans 8:9-11). The depth of this truth with all its implications is difficult to discern. The believing community is the place where each Christian lives and experiences the lordship of Jesus. Thus, life in Christ is not an escape from, nor the absence of, discipleship. It is a walk with a just and correct style of living.

In 2 Corinthians 3:17, and from the perspective of the new covenant, Paul says, "the Lord is the Spirit." That is, the lordship of Jesus begins the new era of salvation. This is the gospel. In the liberty of his Spirit, we are transformed from glory to glory, even though this treasure within us is in earthen vessels (2 Corinthians 4:7). By means of his Spirit, the lordship of Christ is made real and evident. The truth of Calvary and the power of the Spirit show the Christian that his proclamation promotes a new era in which the justice of God rules.

An Obedient Disciple. This expression defines more precisely the person who evangelizes. The task is given because he or she is a follower of Jesus, a disciple who follows the Lord in obedience. This obedience marks the difference between living as a nominal Christian in our cultural context and living in faith within the guidelines of the kingdom of God.

What does obedience in evangelism mean? Or better yet, how is the Christian who evangelizes obedient? To answer this question, we must choose the spirituality of following Christ and the meaning of faith.

First, *the obedient disciple does not proclaim self.* The believer is not the center of the message. The message is Christ, who died and rose again. Neither does the disciple look for privileges. Rather, out of obedience to the Lord each believer serves all classes of all people, with special regard for the most underprivileged.

Second, *the believer does not proclaim the virtues of any one church.* The believer lives discipleship within the bounds of the body of Christ. As a follower of Jesus, he or she does not live alone. Rather, as one of the "living stones," each cooperates with others in love for the extension of the kingdom of God.

Third, *the believer does not bring shame on the Lord.* This truth prohibits the disciple from evading the task of promoting justice in contexts of oppression. Rather than bringing shame on the Lord, the disciple becomes an example of upright living.

Justice as a Challenge for the One Who Evangelizes

This last section of the chapter affirms that justice is done in love. This love makes Christlike the attitudes of the believer before the majority of men and women who now suffer.

As we continue to reflect upon justice as the key in evangelism, upon the evangelizer, questions such as these arise: What happens in the life of one who proclaims Jesus through evangelical actions? If the believer lets the Spirit guide his or her discipleship, how does this affect life? And more, is each reaffirmed in faith? Is there a newness in the one who evangelizes, as there is in the person evangelized? Have we done all that is to be said and done, or is there more to discover in the Christian practice? Furthermore, what makes the one who evangelizes take part in the cause of those who suffer? Do we, for a moment, become a lawyer, a consoler, a defender of the weak?

Perhaps the believer gives the impression that words are the only truth on the earth and what is said exhausts the gospel. With the guidance of the Spirit, one must rid oneself of all evidence of pride, of any trace of being a know-it-all. Some evangelists and missionaries act irresponsibly by speaking of the gospel to those who suffer injustices, while they say nothing of those who foment so much misery and oppression. Also, mission boards establish ministries among poor people in impoverished countries. Then they act undiscerningly by allowing the missionaries to live the comfortable, satisfied, middle-class life of their wealthy homelands. They do not even try to denounce the unjust structures and processes that, from their own homelands, create dependence and all kinds of violence.

In the work of evangelism, the Christian who lives justly in God will inevitably experience the scandal of the cross. Paul calls this the foolishness of the gospel: that God in Christ has chosen for the weak of the world, for those who have been losers—the exploited, the nonpersons. The meeting point between justice and a holistic evangelism is found in Christ and his cross. God chose the weak, the foolish, and the despised to the shame of the wise, the strong, and the powerful (1 Corinthians 1:18-31).

Paul noted that the foolishness or the absurdity of the message of the cross is the power of God for the Christian. Without a doubt, this inversion of values is only possible through God who upsets the unjust order and the imbalance of every lost person. God offers this justice through the most unlikely and least expected means. Luke also sees this concern for justice in Mary's song, the "Magnificat" (Luke 1:46-55).

When the evangelizing activity is seen from this view, it produces an absence of personal glory in the evangelizer. No one can boast since everything is done for the greater glory of God.

I should point out two elements that impact the believer as a doer of justice in Jesus.

Just Actions as an Obedient Answer to Jesus. We have seen that the obedient disciple follows the commands of the Lord. Thus, all one's actions as an evangelizer cause him or her to follow Jesus without any intentions of manipulating anyone. We will, of course, take into consideration social, political, and cultural realities in living and proclaiming the good news.

The words and actions of Jesus energize believers and give their testimony power in a hostile world. Though tempted to hide their identity as believers, they take for their testimony the words of Peter and John: "We cannot but speak of what we have seen and heard" (Acts 4:20). Each is a voice for God before all personal and social injustice, not for personal gain, but because the Lord has elected each (John 15:16). Only then does the Pauline expression "I can do all things through Christ who strengthens me" (Philippians 4:13) take on its correct meaning.

Again we see, from another point of view, that Christ empowers the evangelistic activity. Remember when Jesus sent his disciples he always gave them the resource of his authority and power:

1. They were with him and he gave them authority (Mark 3:13ff.).

2. He sent them two by two with the authority of the Lord (Luke 10:1,19).

3. He sent them as the Father sent him, and he gave them the Spirit (John 20:21-22).

4. They received the task and the promise of the Spirit (Acts 1:8).

5. He sent them with his authority to make disciples (Matthew 28:18-20).

Learnings for the Evangelizer's Own Life. If evangelization is the result of combining both words and deeds, then the one who evangelizes will also be affected by the good news. In situations of injustice, a message from the neighbor and from the unjust situation changes the evangelist's life as well.

Through dialogue, counsel, and friendship, the message-bearer learns lessons, both from the Lord and from others. In viewing the actual situation of the person, each discovers new avenues for sharing life in love. Each identifies ways and means to know how and where to help.

An attitude of humility, as previously stated, will help the evangelizer to remember that the whole truth of the gospel may not yet be clear in each situation. Such an attitude provides space to learn from others. God can then teach each something new through those being evangelized.

Is it possible that learning from the ones being evangelized can create an awakening of the Spirit in the community of believers? Yes, the presence of new believers revitalizes a congregation. They become evangelizers of petrified Christians who are insensitive to another's pain.

Such lifeless believers, installed in their religious rituals, "have left their first love," as Revelation 2:1ff. says.

The one who receives the good news is not only the unconverted. In the process, the Christian also receives the gospel. Both are mutually evangelized, according to their personal needs. It is interesting to note that Paul in Ephesians addresses himself to both Jews and Gentiles. The Jews believed themselves to be saved because they considered themselves descendants of Abraham, the people of God. To the Jews, the Gentiles were excluded from this blessing. Nevertheless, Paul tells the two groups that Jesus came, and he evangelized them both: those who were far off and those who were near (Ephesians 2:17). Thus, those near are also evangelized by those far off, by those who live on the border, on the edges, on the outskirts of an insensitive and unjust society.

Many times Christians behave as if they have the gospel in their pocket, like a passport to heaven. This is why any act of justice has little or no value in their relationship with God. For them, to live justly or not to live justly is the same thing. They consider their salvation so close at hand that they feel no need to receive more of the gospel.

In Spain, I began to understand that I continue being evangelized. The evangelization task is not just going in one direction. It is not from above, going down, from one who supposedly has all the final answers to all the problems of humanity. As an evangelizer, I too am reached by the gospel. I am evangelized.

This truth came to me one cold March morning in 1986. That day I went to visit some families in a neighborhood of miserable hovels, surrounded by elegant new highrise buildings. The construction companies had been ousting these residents to make way for new condominiums. Also at this site, the city is opening a superhighway. As I walked the abandoned sidewalks of the neighborhood, I thought of the family our congregation had helped with food and clothing. They had lost everything in the latest fire, intentionally set to encourage evacuation. They even lost their baby in the fire.

Here and there along these narrow streets of a once-pretty, homey neighborhood, I saw only ashes. One family literally had the heavens for their roof, and lived in the open air on this freezing March day. Then I arrived at Pedro's. He was building his house again, if it could be called that. He told me, "There have been 17 fires," and twice his home was burned. In this last fire, they couldn't even save their nine-month-old child. I knew that in the wealthy sectors, just a few meters from where Pedro hoped to build a shelter again for his family, the dogs and other animals have better dwellings than these families. Where is justice?

The helplessness of my neighbor in that moment moved every fiber of my being. "Hope is the last thing I can lose," Pedro told me. I have heard this same expression in other cultures, and in the same context of injustice and misery. Pedro's experience sharpened the meaning of hope for me. I felt indicted. I had the gospel demonstrated to me by this suffering father. His hope, which is the hope of the poor, evangelized me.

Returning home, I understood that to go to others, to the needy, has a circular dimension. The one who evangelizes gives, but also receives. When the evangelist comes to a group in need of ministry, they send him or her back with a new vision of the glorious reality of the kingdom of God. A reversal of roles takes place—the evangelizer is evangelized.

Believers, as agents of evangelism, see their own faith grow. They feel they mature because they carry on a tangible dialogue with the new believer. Their faith is confirmed in a renewed testimony. This was the experience of the apostle Peter. In Acts 10:1ff., Peter announces the gospel to the Gentile Cornelius. He is converted. But in the process, Peter is also converted. Someone will say, "That cannot be, because Peter is an apostle, and he already was saved." That is true. But Peter's insight shows that the concept of the gospel is not limited to our own understandings, nor is it one-sided. Peter exclaimed, "Truly, I understand that God does not show partiality."

In this experience, he discovered a new dimension of the gospel. He is reevangelized, if you will, and enters into a new phase of his life in dialogue with those who were not Jews. He changed his attitude regarding the Gentiles, those "far off." Now he was ready to accept "the least of these" into the kingdom of God.

---

1. See *Rich Christians in an Age of Hunger: A Biblical Study* by Ronald J. Sider. Downers Grove: InterVarsity Press, 1977, pp. 33f. Also, "Repression and Revolution in Central America," by Hugo Zorrilla. The *Mennonite Quarterly Review Supplement*, August 1984, pp. 335ff. and "Origen de la Riqueza Actual de los Ricos," by Julio de Santa Ana. *Concilium*, No. 207, Septiembre, 1986, pp. 169-186.

Conclusion

The way of the gospel and the way of justice cannot be separated. As faithful disciples of the Lord, we must therefore hold them together in our pilgrimage.

Putting justice into practice on behalf of those who need the whole gospel strengthens faith. In this practice of justice, Christians actively take part in the compassionate acts of God. This will make more compassionate a faith that sometimes seems abstract and evasive.

It is not uncommon to hear someone say that "we should preach the gospel and not get mixed up in social work." Others will confirm this idea with "the Lord called us to proclaim the good news and not waste time in things of this world."

In Germany, during the times of Hitler, Dietrich Bonhoeffer affirmed, "We wrestle for the church of Christ, therefore, we do not get involved in politics." He thereby expressed his opposition to the way in which the Nazi state manipulated Christians. He and his friends discovered, nevertheless, that theirs was also a political stand, evasive and lacking in Christian concern.

Later on, Bonhoeffer wrote to his friends about how such a neutral position would affect future generations. He then looked for "a church for the others," an expression of profound commitment. With this, he made clear that his Christian choice was with those who suffered under the politics of an oppressor state. His choice of a church for the service of those who suffer cost him his life.

Today, many Christians in democratic countries believe voting is a way to express concern for justice. They vote for candidates they believe will help to correct injustices in their society. Some Christians even run for political office. They want to work for justice through government structures, be they local, regional, or national offices. Becoming active in the political process, however, does not mean support for, nor involvement in unchristian activities. Lying, deceit, or other dishonest means have no place in a Christian's life.

Finally, I believe this study has shown that God looks for just and fair actions. These are in accord with his plan for the life of human beings. The experience of knowing God through faith in Christ then leads to just and upright living. This finds its meaning in doing the will of the Father. Thus, the believer is converted into one who practices justice in sacrificial love.

All evangelistic efforts have to begin and end with the justice of God. This justice is a "declaration," or gift of God. We are made just through faith. We do not need to earn it. But justice is also a result of the power of God. God's power enables us to live justly, to do what is right toward others. So God's justice is gift and service. It is to be just and to act justly toward others. It is liberty and obedience in Christ for the disciple. Both truths are inseparable. Whether gift or declaration, it has the character of obedience. No gift exists that is not given to the Christian to use. There is no service in Christ that does not bring the gift of salvation near.

Complementary Readings

Driver, John. *Community and Commitment*, Scottdale: Herald Press, 1976.

Jacobs, Donald. *Pilgrimage in Mission*, Scottdale: Herald Press, 1983.

Sider, Ronald J. *Rich Christians in an Age of Hunger: A Biblical Study.* Downers Grove: InterVarsity Press, 1977.

Toews, John E., and Gordon Nickel. *The Power of the Lamb*, Hillsboro: Kindred Press, 1986.

The Author

Hugo Zorrilla is a Colombian by birth. He received his Bachelor of Theology from the Latin America Biblical Seminary of San Jose, Costa Rica. He received a Masters degree in New Testament from Trinity Divinity School in Deerfield, Illinois, a Bachelor's degree in Classical Philology from the University of Costa Rica, and a Doctorate in Theology from the Pontifical University of Salamanca, Spain.

He has been a pastor in Colombia and Costa Rica, professor and dean at the Biblical Seminary in Costa Rica, and visiting professor at the Mennonite Brethren Seminary in Fresno, California. He is the author of various articles and books on discipleship.

Hugo presently works in Madrid, Spain, as a missionary with the Mennonite Brethren church. This ministry includes pastoral work and the production of discipleship materials.

He and his wife, Norma Esther, have three children: Ruth, Andres, and Ana.

PEACE AND JUSTICE SERIES

Edited by Elizabeth Showalter and J. Allen Brubaker

This series of books sets forth briefly and simply some important emphases of the Bible concerning war and peace and how to deal with conflict and injustice. The authors write from a perspective rooted in the Anabaptist heritage of the sixteenth century. This includes a holistic view of the Scriptures and a belief that the believing community discerns God's word for today through the guidance of the Spirit. Some of the titles reflect biblical, theological, or historical content. Other titles in the series show how these principles and insights are lived out in daily life.

1. *The Way God Fights* by Lois Barrett
2. *How Christians Made Peace With War* by John Driver
3. *They Loved Their Enemies* by Marian Hostetler
4. *The Good News of Justice* by Hugo Zorrilla
5. *Freedom for the Captives* by Jose Gallardo
6. *When Kingdoms Clash* by Calvin E. Shenk
7. *Do Justice* by Lois Barrett

The books in this series are published in North America by:

Herald Press
616 Walnut Avenue
Scottdale, PA 15683
USA

Herald Press
117 King Street, West
Kitchener, ON N2G 4M5
CANADA

Overseas persons wanting copies for distribution or permission to translate should write to the Scottdale address listed above.